Master your German vocabulary with CGP!

There are lots of words to learn for GCSE German, but never fear. This small but mighty Vocabulary Book will see you through!

It covers every word on the AQA course, all arranged by topic — and it's marked up for Higher and Foundation tiers too.

We've also included handy Sentence Builders to help you put the vocab into practice — you can thank us later!

CGP — still the best! ☺

Our sole aim here at CGP is to produce the highest quality books — carefully written, immaculately presented and dangerously close to being funny.

Then we work our socks off to get them out to you — at the cheapest possible prices.

Contents

Section Ten — Media and Technology

Section Eleven — Where People Live

Section Twelve — Environmental and Social Issues

Section Thirteen — Nouns, Cases and Linking Words

Section Fourteen — Adjectives and Adverbs

Published by CGP

Editors: Rebecca Greaves, Lorna Kimmins, Nathan Leach, Ali Palin

With thanks to Margit Grassick, Rose Jones and Suzanne Rose for the proofreading.
With thanks to Alice Dent for the copyright research.

ISBN: 978 1 83774 214 1

Printed by Elanders Ltd, Newcastle upon Tyne.
Clipart from Corel®

Based on the classic CGP style created by Richard Parsons.

General Stuff

Numbers

die Nummer	*number*
die Zahl	*number*
null	*zero*
eins	*one*
zwei	*two*
drei	*three*
vier	*four*
fünf	*five*
sechs	*six*
sieben	*seven*
acht	*eight*
neun	*nine*
zehn	*ten*
elf	*eleven*
zwölf	*twelve*
dreizehn	*thirteen*
vierzehn	*fourteen*
fünfzehn	*fifteen*
sechzehn	*sixteen*
siebzehn	*seventeen*
achtzehn	*eighteen*
neunzehn	*nineteen*
zwanzig	*twenty*
dreißig	*thirty*
vierzig	*forty*
fünfzig	*fifty*
sechzig	*sixty*
siebzig	*seventy*
achtzig	*eighty*
neunzig	*ninety*
hundert	*hundred*
tausend	*thousand*
eine Million, Mio	*million*
erste	*first*
die Menge	*quantity, amount*
die Hälfte	*half*
der Teil	*piece*
zuerst	*first (of all)*
einzig	*only, single*
ein bisschen	*a little*
einige	*a few, some*
viel	*a lot*
viele	*a lot, many*
wenig	*little*
wenige	*few*
alle	*all*
ungefähr	*approximately, about*
ganz	*whole, all the*
der Meter, m	*metre*
der Zentimeter, cm	*centimetre, cm*
das Prozent	*percent*

Higher

die Anzahl	*quantity, number (count, amount)*
der Rest	*rest, remainder*
zählen	*to count*

Higher

übrig	*remaining, left, leftover, spare*
weitere	*additional, further, another*
einzeln	*individual, single, separately*
insgesamt	*in all, in total, altogether, overall*

Times

die Zeit	*time*
die Stunde	*hour*
die Minute	*minute*
die Sekunde	*second*
Uhr	*o'clock*
Viertel	*quarter*
halb	*half*
vor	*before*
nach	*after*
der Moment	*moment, instant*
der Morgen	*morning*
der Mittag	*noon, midday*
der Nachmittag	*afternoon*
der Abend	*evening*
die Nacht	*night*
dauern	*to last, take (time)*

Higher

der Zeitpunkt	*moment, (point in) time*
geschehen	*to happen, occur, take place*

Dates

Montag	*Monday*
Dienstag	*Tuesday*
Mittwoch	*Wednesday*
Donnerstag	*Thursday*
Freitag	*Friday*
Samstag	*Saturday*
Sonntag	*Sunday*
der Frühling	*spring*
der Sommer	*summer*
der Herbst	*autumn*
der Winter	*winter*
Januar	*January*
Februar	*February*
März	*March*
April	*April*
Mai	*May*
Juni	*June*
Juli	*July*
August	*August*
September	*September*
Oktober	*October*
November	*November*
Dezember	*December*
der Tag	*day*
die Woche	*week*
das Wochenende	*weekend*
der Monat	*month*
das Jahr	*year*
das Mal	*time (occurrence)*

der Anfang	*beginning, start*
der Beginn	*beginning, start*
das Ende	*end, finish*
die Vergangenheit	*past*
die Zukunft	*future*
H das Jahrhundert	*century*
H die Gegenwart	*present*

Time Phrases

gestern	*yesterday*
neulich	*recently, lately, the other day*
früher	*previously, in former times, in the past*
in letzter Zeit	*recently, lately*
heute	*today*
jetzt	*now, currently*
gleich	*straight away, right away, immediately*
sofort	*immediately*
morgen	*tomorrow*
endlich	*finally, at last, eventually*
schließlich	*finally, at last, eventually*
danach	*afterwards*
immer	*always*
oft	*often, frequently*
täglich	*daily, every day*
regelmäßig	*regular, regularly*
bald	*soon*

manchmal	*sometimes*
nochmal	*again*
noch	*still, yet, else*
ab und zu	*now and again, (every) now and then*
selten	*rare, rarely*
einmal	*once*
nie	*never*
inzwischen	*in the meantime, meanwhile*
dann	*then*
damals	*then, at that time, in those days*
diesmal	*this time*
diese	*this, that*
jede	*each, every*
nächste	*next*
letzte	*last*
Higher: gerade	*just now, right now*
Higher: häufig	*frequent, frequently, often*
Higher: ständig	*constant, permanent, constantly, permanently*
Higher: jährlich	*annually*

Questions

die Frage	*question, query*
ja	*yes*
nein, nee, nö	*no*
okay	*okay*
ach	*oh*

was?	*what?*
wann?	*when?*
wo?	*where?*
warum?	*why?*
wie?	*how?*
wie viele?	*how many?*
wohin?	*where...to?*
woher?	*where...from?*
wer / wem / wen?	*who / whom?*
welche?	*which (one)?*
was für?	*what sort / type of…?*
H wieso?	*why?*

Being Polite

hallo	*hello, hi*
guten Morgen	*good morning*
guten Tag	*good afternoon*
guten Abend	*good evening*
willkommen	*welcome*
auf Wiedersehen	*goodbye*
bis bald	*bye for now, see you soon*
tschüss	*bye*
es geht mir... gut / schlecht	*I am… fine, well / not well*
ich möchte	*I would like*
bitte	*please, you're welcome*
danke	*thanks*
das geht	*that's fine, that's possible*
alles klar	*all right, that's fine, okay, understood*
es tut mir leid	*I'm sorry*
die Entschuldigung	*apology, excuse*
Entschuldigung	*sorry, excuse me*
entschuldigen	*to excuse*
sich entschuldigen (bei)	*to apologise (to)*
Herr	*Mr.*
Frau	*Mrs.*
die Dame	*lady*

Higher

die Vorstellung	*introduction, idea*
vorstellen	*to introduce*
danken	*to thank*
herzlich	*cordial, warm, warmly*

Opinions — Giving Your Opinion

die Meinung	*opinion, view*
meiner Meinung nach	*in my opinion*
meinen	*to think, have an opinion*
denken (an)	*to think (of)*
finden	*to find*
erzählen (von)	*to tell (about)*
diskutieren (über)	*to discuss (+ noun)*

gern, gerne	*gladly, like to (+ verb)*
mögen	*to like*
genießen	*to enjoy*
lieben	*to love*
hassen	*to hate, detest*
freuen	*to please, make happy*
sich freuen	*to be happy / pleased*
sich freuen auf	*to look forward to*
sich interessieren (für)	*to be interested (in)*
egal	*(it's all) the same, indifferent, doesn't matter*
es ist mir egal	*I don't care*
es kommt darauf an, ob...	*it depends whether...*
schade	*(it's a) pity, (it's a) shame*
der Grund	*reason, basis*

Higher

halten ... für	*to think of ... as*
von ... her	*as far as ... is concerned*
der Gegensatz	*opposite, contrast*
das Gegenteil	*opposite*

Opinions — Adjectives and Adverbs

gut	*good, well*
schlecht	*bad, badly*
perfekt	*perfect, perfectly*
fantastisch	*fantastic, super, terrific*
toll	*great, amazing*
interessant	*interesting*
lustig	*funny, enjoyable*
wichtig	*important*
wunderbar	*wonderful*
klar	*clear, obvious*
ideal	*ideal*
schrecklich	*terrible, awful, dreadful, terribly, awfully, dreadfully*
blöd	*stupid, dumb*
schlimm	*bad, serious*
langweilig	*boring*
einfach	*easy, easily, simple, simply*
schwierig	*difficult, hard, tough*
extrem	*extreme, extremely*
wahr	*true, real, genuine*
falsch	*false, wrong*
schnell	*quickly, fast*
langsam	*slow, slowly*
voll	*full, complete*
leer	*empty*
kurz	*short, brief*

Higher

notwendig	*necessary*
super	*super*
wert	*worth, worthy of*

Higher

zufrieden	*satisfied, happy, content*
ungewöhnlich	*unusual, unusually*
unglaublich	*unbelievable, incredible, unbelievably*
verrückt	*crazy, insane, mad*

Opinions — Giving Reasons

weil	*because*
denn	*because*
auch	*also, too, as well*
also	*so, therefore*
deshalb	*therefore*
deswegen	*for this reason, therefore*
zum Beispiel, z.B.	*for example, e.g.*
und so weiter, usw.	*and so on, etc.*
dagegen	*on the other hand*
auf der einen / anderen Seite	*on the one / other hand*
jedoch	*however*
trotzdem	*nevertheless*
insbesondere	*especially, particularly*
offensichtlich	*obvious, obviously*

Higher

selbstverständlich	*natural, self-evident, obvious, naturally, obviously*

Higher

statt ... zu	*instead of ...*
um ... zu	*in order to ...*
ohne ... zu	*without ...*

Useful Nouns

das Ding	*thing, object*
die Sache	*thing, matter*
die Art	*type, kind, sort*
das Beispiel	*example, instance*
das Mittel	*means, average*
das Thema	*topic, theme*
die Themen	*topics, themes*
die Idee	*idea*
die Lust	*desire*
der Unterschied	*difference*
der Vergleich	*comparison*
die Sicherheit	*certainty*
der Hintergrund	*background*
der Punkt	*dot, point, full stop*

Higher

die Tatsache	*fact*
die Wahrheit	*truth*
der Gedanke	*thought, idea*
das Konzept	*concept, idea, plan*
die Ahnung	*suspicion, idea*
der Eindruck	*impression, effect*
die Weise	*way, manner*
die Alternative	*alternative*
die Änderung	*change, modification, alteration*

Higher

der Vorschlag	*suggestion, proposal*
die Entscheidung	*decision*
der Ausdruck	*term, expression*
die Bedeutung	*meaning, significance*
der Sinn	*sense, meaning*
der Wert	*value, worth*
der Zweck	*purpose, aim*
die Beschreibung	*description*
der Schluss	*end, conclusion, finish, closure*
der Titel	*title*
die Liste	*list*
die Reihe	*row, line, queue*
die Hoffnung	*hope*
der Zweifel	*doubt*
das Gute	*the good thing*
etwas Nettes	*something nice*

Useful Adjectives and Adverbs

anders	*different, differently*
besonders	*particularly, especially*
bestimmt	*certain, definite, certainly, definitely*
ehemalig	*former*
einmal	*once*
fast	*almost, nearly*
fest	*firm, solid, steady*
ganz	*quite*
gar	*at all*
genau	*exact, exactly, precise, precisely*
genauso	*just as*
genug	*enough*
irgendwann	*sometime, someday*
irgendwie	*somehow*
irgendwo	*somewhere*
los	*rid of, going on*
meist	*most, mostly, usually*
möglich	*possible*
natürlich	*of course, certainly*
nochmal	*again*
normalerweise	*normally, usually*
nur	*only, just*
offenbar	*apparent, obvious, apparently, obviously*
plötzlich	*sudden, suddenly*
sicher	*certain, sure, of course*
total	*total, complete, totally, completely*
typisch	*typical, typically*

vielleicht	*perhaps, maybe, possibly*
wahrscheinlich	*likely, probable, probably*
wieder	*again*
wirklich	*real, actual, really, actually, truly*
wohl	*well, probably, arguably*
ziemlich	*quite, fairly, pretty*

Higher

absolut	*absolute, complete, absolutely, completely*
allgemein	*general*
alles (Andere)	*everything (else)*
bereit	*ready*
deutlich	*clear, clearly*
eigentlich	*actual, real, actually, really*
entfernt	*distant, away*
gerade	*straight, just, just now, right now*
gering	*low, small*
hoffentlich	*hopefully*
individuell	*individual, individually*
künstlich	*artificial, artificially*
niedrig	*low*
relativ	*relative, relatively, comparatively*
sogenannt	*so-called*
tief	*deep, low*
unterschiedlich	*different, varied, variable, diverse*
verschieden	*different, various, diverse*
vollständig	*complete, completely, thoroughly*
völlig	*completely, absolutely*

Useful Verbs

sein	*to be*
haben	*to have*
werden	*to become*
beginnen	*to begin, start*
enden	*to end, finish*
brauchen	*to need, use*
benutzen	*to use*
sehen	*to see, watch*
holen	*to get, fetch*
bringen	*to bring*
kriegen	*to get, receive*
tun	*to do, put*
stellen	*to place, set, put*
sich stellen	*to place oneself, stand*
ziehen	*to pull, move*
zeigen	*to show, point*
sprechen	*to speak, talk*
bedeuten	*to mean*

verändern	*to change*
versuchen	*to try*
wollen	*to want (to)*
können	*to be able to, can*
hoffen (auf)	*to hope (for)*
sich erinnern	*to remember*
gehen	*to go*
gehen um	*to be about*
verdienen	*to deserve*
scheinen	*to seem, shine, appear*
wissen	*to know (something)*
vergessen	*to forget*
erinnern (an)	*to remind (about)*

Higher

bemerken	*to notice*
merken	*to notice*
sich [dat.] merken	*to remember*
denken (an)	*to think (of)*
sich [dat.] denken	*to imagine*
bestehen (auf [dat.])	*to insist (on)*
bestehen (aus)	*to consist (of)*
nachdenken	*to think about, reflect*
vergleichen (mit)	*to compare*
legen	*to lay, put*

Higher

überlegen	*to consider, think about, think of*
sich handeln um	*to be about*
sich drehen um	*to be about*
entstehen	*to originate, develop*
entwickeln	*to develop*
schaffen	*to create, manage, accomplish*
ändern	*to change, alter*
überzeugen	*to convince, persuade*
annehmen	*to accept, assume*
verlangen	*to request, demand*
bitten um	*to request, ask for*
rufen	*to call, shout*
beschließen	*to decide*
erfahren	*to experience, find out*
reichen	*to reach, be enough*
gehören	*to belong*
erwarten	*to expect*
aufmachen	*to open*
setzen	*to set, place, put*

Sentence Builder — Days and Times

Today's the day — it's time to make some sentences about your weekend.

Have a go at this question: **'Was machst du normalerweise samstags?'**

Example: Samstags esse ich mein Frühstück und bald danach gehe ich laufen. Letzten Samstag habe ich einen Film gesehen, der toll war, weil ich mit meinen Freunden dort war. Morgen möchte ich in die Stadt fahren, aber es kommt darauf an, ob ich Zeit habe.

Samstags *On Saturdays,*	stehe ich früh auf *I get up early*	und bald danach *and soon after*	gehe ich laufen. *I go running.*
Normalerweise *Normally*	schlafe ich bis neun Uhr *I sleep until nine o'clock*	und um halb zwölf *and at half past eleven*	treffe ich mich mit meinen Freunden. *I meet up with my friends.*
Am Morgen *In the morning,*	esse ich mein Frühstück *I eat my breakfast*	H: und sobald ich bereit bin, *and as soon as I am ready*	

Letzten Samstag *Last Saturday,*	habe ich einen Film gesehen, der *I saw a film that*	toll war, *was great*	weil ich mit meinen Freunden dort war. *because I was there with my friends.*
Letztes Wochenende *Last weekend,*	bin ich zu einem Konzert gegangen, das *I went to a concert that*	H: mir wirklich gefallen hat, *I really liked*	aber dagegen war das Ticket teuer. *but on the other hand, the ticket was expensive.*

Nächsten Samstag *Next Saturday,*	möchte ich *I would like*	mehr Sport treiben, *to do more sport,*	aber es kommt darauf an, ob *but it depends whether*	ich Zeit habe. *I have time.*
Morgen *Tomorrow,*	H: würde ich gern *I would like*	in die Stadt fahren, *to go into town,*		das Wetter gut ist. *the weather is good.*
Diesen Monat *This month,*		an den Strand gehen, *to go to the beach,*		

I think my clock is hungry — it went back four seconds...

One way to liven up your opinions is to include adjectives — try to go beyond 'gut' and 'schlecht' and add some pizzazz with words like 'fantastisch' and 'schrecklich'.

Identity & Relationships with Others

About Yourself

der Name	*name*
heißen	*to be called*
das Alter	*age*
der Geburtstag	*birthday*
geboren	*born*
-jährig	*years old*
wohnen	*to live*
englisch	*English*
deutsch	*German*
europäisch	*European*
französisch	*French*
spanisch	*Spanish*
hetero(sexuell)	*straight*
bi(sexuell)	*bi, bisexual*
gay	*gay*
trans(gender)	*transgender*
nicht binär, nichtbinär	*non-binary*
die Religion	*religion*
der / die Christ(in)	*Christian*
der Muslim	*Muslim (m)*
die Muslime	*Muslim (f)*
der Jude	*Jewish (m), Jewish person*
die Jüdin	*Jewish (f)*
der / die Hindu	*Hindu*
der Deutsche	*the German (m)*
ein Deutscher	*a German (m)*
die Deutsche	*the German (f)*
eine Deutsche	*a German (f)*
Deutsche	*Germans*
die Deutschen	*the Germans*

Higher

die Geburt	*birth*
britisch	*British*
österreichisch	*Austrian*
türkisch	*Turkish*
Schweizer	*Swiss*
Berliner	*(of) Berlin*
vorstellen	*to introduce*
nennen	*to name, call*
sich nennen	*to be called*
stammen aus	*to come from*

My Family and Friends

die Familie	*family*
das Mitglied	*member*
die Person	*person*
der Mensch	*human being, person*
die Eltern (pl)	*parents*
die Geschwister (pl)	*siblings*
das Kind	*child*
das Einzelkind	*only child*

der Vater	*father*
die Mutter	*mother*
der Sohn	*son*
die Tochter	*daughter*
der Bruder	*brother*
die Brüder (pl)	*brothers*
die Schwester	*sister*
die Großeltern (pl)	*grandparents*
der Opa	*grandpa, grandad, grandfather*
die Oma	*grandma, grandmother*
der Onkel	*uncle*
die Tante	*aunt*
der Cousin	*cousin (m)*
die Cousine	*cousin (f)*
Stief-	*step-*
das Tier	*animal*
der Hund	*dog*
die Katze	*cat*
der Vogel	*bird*
das Pferd	*horse*
der / die Erwachsene	*adult, grown-up*
der Junge	*boy*
das Mädchen	*girl*
der / die Nachbar(in)	*neighbour*
der / die Betreuer(in)	*carer*
der / die Jugendliche	*young person, adolescent*

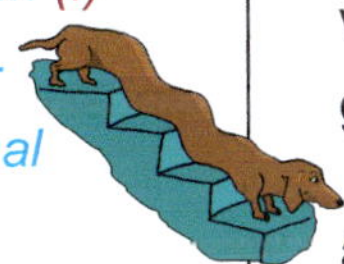

der Typ	*bloke, guy*
der Freund	*male friend*
die Freundin	*female friend*
beste	*best*
eng	*close*
sprechen	*to speak, talk*
sagen	*to say, tell*
kennen	*to know*
kennenlernen, kennen lernen	*to meet (for first time), get to know*
anrufen	*to ring, phone*
treffen	*to meet*
sich treffen	*to meet up*
verbringen	*to spend (time)*
lachen	*to laugh*
lächeln	*to smile*
verstehen	*to understand*
gemeinsam	*common, mutual, in common, joint*
ähnlich	*similar, similarly*
gute / schlechte Laune haben	*to be in a good / bad mood*
das Gespräch	*conversation, talk*

Higher

die Generation	*generation*
die Jugend	*youth*
pflegen	*to care for, nurse, cultivate (e.g. a friendship)*
sich unterhalten	*to chat*

Appearances

beschreiben	*to describe*
aussehen	*to appear, look*
das Gesicht	*face*
das Haar	*hair*
das Auge	*eye*
die Größe	*size, height*
groß	*big, tall*
klein	*small, little, short*
dick	*fat*
schlank	*slim, thin*
kurz	*short*
lang	*long*
rund	*round*
jung	*young*
alt	*old*
die Farbe	*colour*
rot	*red*
gelb	*yellow*
grün	*green*
blau	*blue*
braun	*brown*
grau	*grey*
schwarz	*black*
weiß	*white*
hell	*light, bright*
dunkel	*dark*
schön	*lovely, beautiful*
schauen	*to look*

Higher

dünn	*thin*
hässlich	*ugly, hideous*
hübsch	*pretty, cute, lovely*
die Brille	*(pair of) glasses*
die Tätowierung	*tattoo, tattooing*
der Ausdruck	*expression*
erkennen	*to recognise, admit, realise*

Personalities

die Persönlichkeit	*personality*
freundlich	*kind, nice, friendly*
glücklich	*happy, fortunate, happily*
froh	*happy, glad*
nett	*nice*
ehrlich	*honest*
geduldig	*patient*
positiv	*positive*
lieb	*dear, kind*
süß	*sweet, cute*
hilfsbereit	*helpful, cooperative*
witzig	*funny, witty, comical*
höflich	*polite*
ruhig	*quiet, calm*
kreativ	*creative, creatively*
sportlich	*sporty, athletic*
negativ	*negative*
traurig	*sad*
böse	*bad, mad, naughty, angry*

komisch	*funny, comical, strange, odd, weird*
ernst	*serious*
faul	*lazy, idle*
streng	*strict, severe*
unabhängig	*independent*
gemein	*mean, cruel, nasty*
peinlich	*embarrassing, awkward*
ärgerlich	*annoying, irritating*
sich verlieren	*to get lost (in thought)*

Higher

großzügig	*generous*
hilfreich	*helpful*
stolz	*proud*
frech	*cheeky, naughty*
eifersüchtig	*jealous*
die Eigenschaft	*quality, characteristic, trait*
sich verhalten	*to behave, act*

Relationships and Partnerships

die Beziehung	*relation, relationship*
sich verstehen mit	*to get on well with*
auskommen mit	*to get on with*
der Streit	*argument, fight, dispute*
streiten	*to quarrel, argue, dispute*
helfen	*to help*
hören auf	*to hear, listen, to listen to, obey someone*
unterstützen	*to support*
die Unterstützung	*support*
versprechen	*to promise*
jemandem auf die Nerven gehen	*to get on someone's nerves*
sorgen	*to care, worry*
sich kümmern um	*to take care of, concerned about*
fehlen	*to be missing*
das Paar	*pair, couple*
der Partner	*partner*
das Gefühl	*feeling*
die Liebe	*love*
lieben	*to love*
ledig	*single, unmarried*
zusammen	*together, altogether*
allein, alleine	*alone*
miteinander	*with each other*
getrennt	*separated*
die Ehe	*marriage*
heiraten	*to marry*
verheiratet	*married*
die Hochzeit	*wedding, marriage*
die zivile Partnerschaft	*civil partnership*

der Mann	*husband, man*
die Frau	*wife, woman*
geschieden	*divorced*
vertrauen (Higher)	*to trust*
halten ... für (Higher)	*to think of ... as*
kritisieren (Higher)	*to criticise*
enttäuschen (Higher)	*to disappoint, frustrate*
stören (Higher)	*to disturb, bother*
der Konflikt (Higher)	*conflict, dispute*
gegenseitig (Higher)	*mutual, each other*
sich trennen (Higher)	*to separate*
das Verständnis (Higher)	*understanding, sympathy*
die Erinnerung (Higher)	*memory*

Sentence Builder — Your Family

Whether your family are serious or a seriously good laugh, here's how to talk about them.

Have a go at answering this question: **'Wie ist deine Familie?'**

Example: Mein Bruder ist groß und hat braune Augen. Ich verbringe gern Zeit mit meiner Mutter, denn sie ist immer positiv. Meine Beziehung zu meinem Onkel ist gut, da er hilfsbereit und ehrlich ist, jedoch streiten wir uns manchmal.

Mein Vater *My father*	ist *is*	klein *small*	und hat *and has*	braune Augen. *brown eyes.*
Mein Bruder *My brother*		groß *tall*		lange Haare. *long hair.*
Meine Schwester *My sister*		freundlich *friendly*		ein schlankes Gesicht. *a slim face.*
		ernst *serious*		H: Tätowierungen. *tattoos.*

Ich verstehe mich gut mit *I get on well with*	meiner Mutter, *my mother*	denn sie ist *because she is*	immer *always*	nett. *nice.*
Ich verbringe gern Zeit mit *I like spending time with*	meiner Tante, *my aunt*		wirklich *really*	witzig. *funny.*
	meiner Cousine, *my cousin*		sehr *very*	geduldig. *patient.*
				positiv. *positive.*

Meine Beziehung zu meinem Onkel ist gut, *My relationship with my uncle is good*	da er hilfsbereit und ehrlich ist, *as he is helpful and honest,*	jedoch *however*	streiten wir uns manchmal. *sometimes we argue.*
Higher: Ich vertraue meinem Opa, *I trust my grandfather*	weil er mich unterstützt, *because he supports me,*	trotzdem *nevertheless*	kann er streng sein. *he can be strict.*
		H: allerdings *though*	geht er mir oft auf die Nerven. *he often gets on my nerves.*

We used to have a big family tree, but Dad chopped it down...

Now make your own sentences talking about your friends — you could even use the past tense to say what your relationships *were* like when you were younger.

Healthy Living and Lifestyle

Food

das Essen	*food, meal*
essen	*to eat*
trinken	*to drink*
der Hunger	*hunger*
der Durst	*thirst*
kochen	*to cook, boil*
das Gemüse	*vegetables*
das Obst	*fruit*
das Brot	*bread*
der Käse	*cheese*
das Ei	*egg*
die Pommes (frites)	*chips, fries*
das Fleisch	*meat*
das Hähnchen	*chicken*
die Wurst	*sausage*
der Fisch	*fish*
der Zucker	*sugar*
der Kuchen	*cake*
das Eis	*ice, ice cream*
das Wasser	*water*
die Cola	*cola*
die Milch	*milk*
der Kaffee	*coffee*
der Wein	*wine*
das Bier	*beer*
lecker	*tasty, delicious*
süß	*sweet, sugary*
scharf	*spicy, hot*
frisch	*fresh, freshly*
das Frühstück	*breakfast*
das Mittagessen	*lunch*
das Abendessen	*dinner*
nehmen	*to have something to eat or drink*
der Imbiss	*snack, refreshment*
der / die Veganer(in)	*vegan*
der / die Vegetarier(in)	*vegetarian*
das Restaurant	*restaurant*
die Speisekarte, die Karte	*menu*
das Stück	*piece*
die Flasche	*bottle*
das Glas	*glass*
das Kilo(gramm), kg	*kilo, kilogram*
bestellen	*to order*

Higher

das Getränk	*drink*
das Gericht	*dish*
das Produkt	*product*
das Protein	*protein*
schmecken	*to taste*

Healthy Living

die Gesundheit	*health*
gesund	*healthy, healthily*
das Leben	*life*
die Energie	*energy*
bewusst	*conscious, aware*
aufstehen	*to stand up, get up*
stehen	*to stand*
schlafen	*to sleep*
liegen	*to lie, be lying down*
abnehmen	*to lose weight*
zunehmen	*to put on weight*
die Bewegung	*exercise, movement*
der Sport	*sport*
die Aktivität	*activity*
die Fitness	*fitness*
das Fitness-Studio	*gym*
bewegen	*to move*
sich bewegen	*to exercise*
Sport treiben	*to do sport*
in Form sein	*to be in form / good shape*
joggen	*to jog*
laufen	*to run, walk*
schwimmen	*to swim*
spazieren	*to (go for a) walk, stroll*
wandern	*to (go on a) walk / hike, ramble (in the countryside)*
sportlich	*sporty, athletic*
aktiv	*active, energetic*
stark	*strong*
schwach	*weak*
schnell	*quickly, fast*

Higher

die Ernährung	*food, diet, nutrition*
erhalten	*to preserve, maintain*
sich entspannen	*to relax*
einschlafen	*to fall asleep, doze off*
die Turnhalle	*gymnasium*
die Kraft	*strength, power*
die Übung	*exercise*
halten	*to stop, hold, keep*
aufbauen	*to build up*
führen	*to lead*

Unhealthy Living

die Gefahr	*danger, risk, threat*
gefährlich	*dangerous, risky*
der Alkohol	*alcohol*
die Droge	*drug*
das Fastfood	*fast food*
die Zigarette	*cigarette*
rauchen	*to smoke*
vermeiden	*to avoid*
abhängen	*to depend*
betrunken	*drunk*
faul	*lazy, idle*

Higher

die Krise	*crisis*
drohen	*to threaten*
aufgeben	*to give up, quit*
aufhören	*to stop*
übergewichtig	*overweight*
abhängig	*dependent, addicted*
süchtig (nach)	*addicted (to), hooked (on)*
verzichten auf	*to do without*
enthalten	*to contain*

Illnesses and Treatments

die Krankheit	*illness, disease*
krank	*sick, ill*
die Schmerzen	*pains, aches*
die Angst	*fear, anxiety*
die Sorge	*care, worry*
sorgen	*to care*
sich sorgen (um)	*to worry (about)*
müde	*tired*
das Gefühl	*feeling*
fühlen	*to feel (+ noun)*
sich fühlen	*to feel (+ adjective)*
sitzen	*to sit*
verletzen	*to injure, hurt*
leiden (an [dat.])	*to suffer (from)*
leiden (unter [dat.])	*to suffer (as a result of)*
weinen	*to cry*
sterben (an [dat.])	*to die (from)*
tot	*dead*
der Körper	*body*
der Kopf	*head*
der Arm	*arm*
die Hand	*hand*
das Bein	*leg*
der Fuß	*foot*
der Rücken	*back*
das Ohr	*ear*
das Auge	*eye*
der Mund	*mouth*
der Muskel	*muscle*
das Herz	*heart*
der Arzt / die Ärztin	*doctor*
das Krankenhaus	*hospital*
retten	*to save, rescue*
sich kümmern um	*to take care of, be concerned about*
verbessern	*to improve*
empfehlen	*to recommend*

Higher

der Schmerz	pain, ache
der Unfall	accident, crash
körperlich	physical, physically
der Tod	death
töten	to kill
anstrengend	exhausting, strenuous, tiring
spüren	to sense, notice, feel
sich legen	to lie down
sich setzen	to sit down
sich [dat.] brechen	to break (a bone)
die Schulter	shoulder
der Bauch	belly
das Knie	knee
die Knie	knees

Higher

die Haut	skin
die Nase	nose
der Zahn	tooth
der Finger	finger
das Blut	blood
der / die Doktor(in), Dr.	doctor
der / die Patient(in)	patient
die Ursache	reason, cause
der Termin	appointment
das Medikament	medicine
medizinisch	medical
untersuchen	to examine
behandeln	to treat
pflegen	to care, nurse
verbinden	to bandage
verhindern	to prevent
warnen (vor [dat.])	to warn (of / about)

Sentence Builder — Health

Turns out wellness isn't about how much water you can hold... ahem, moving on...

Try answering this question: **'Wie kann man gesund bleiben?'**

Example: In Form sein ist gut für die Gesundheit, deshalb soll man regelmäßig Sport treiben. Man kann auch den Arzt anrufen, wenn man sich um die Gesundheit sorgt. Man soll versuchen, Drogen zu vermeiden, sonst kann man danach süchtig werden.

Bewegung *Exercise*	ist gut für die Gesundheit, *is good for your health,*	also *so*	soll man *you should*	regelmäßig Sport treiben. *do sport regularly.*
In Form sein *Being in good shape*		deshalb *therefore*		
Aktiv sein *Being active*	gibt mehr Energie, *gives you more energy,*	deswegen *therefore*		oft in der Natur spazieren. *go for a stroll in nature often.*

Man kann auch *You can also*	Hilfe bekommen, *get help*	wenn man an einer Krankheit leidet. *if you're suffering from an illness.*
	den Arzt / die Ärztin anrufen, *ring the doctor*	wenn man sich um die Gesundheit sorgt. *if you're concerned about your health.*
	Higher: einen Termin organisieren, *organise an appointment*	Higher: damit man einen Schmerz behandeln kann. *so that a pain can be treated.*
		Higher: um eine körperliche Verletzung untersuchen zu lassen. *in order to have a physical injury examined.*

Higher

Mir ist es wichtig, *It's important to me*	Drogen zu vermeiden, *to avoid drugs*	sonst kann man danach süchtig werden. *otherwise you can get addicted to them.*
Man soll versuchen, *You should try*	Zigaretten aufzugeben, *to give up cigarettes*	
Ich würde es jemandem empfehlen, *I would recommend someone*	auf viel Fastfood und Alkohol zu verzichten, *to do without lots of fast food and alcohol*	die gefährliche Stoffe enthalten. *which contain dangerous substances.*

Does eating a burger on a tightrope count as a balanced diet?

Now have a go at talking about all the things that *you* do to stay healthy, and why.

Education

School Subjects

das Fach	*subject*
das Lieblingsfach	*favourite subject*
die Mathematik, die Mathe	*mathematics, maths*
die Biologie	*biology*
die Chemie	*chemistry*
die Physik	*physics*
die Wissenschaft	*science*
die Technik	*technology*
die Sprache	*language*
das Englisch	*English*
das Deutsch	*German*
das Französisch	*French*
das Spanisch	*Spanish*
die Literatur	*literature*
die Geschichte	*history*
die Erdkunde	*geography*
die Religion	*religion*
die Kunst	*art*
die Musik	*music*
das Theater	*drama*
der Sport	*sport, PE*
das Kochen	*cookery*
leicht	*easy, simple*
einfach	*simple, easy simply, easily*
schwer	*difficult, hard*
schwierig	*difficult, hard, tough*
hart	*hard*
stark	*strong*
schwach	*weak*
wichtig	*important*
praktisch	*practical, useful*
nützlich	*useful*
interessant	*interesting*
langweilig	*boring*
kreativ	*creative, creatively*
musikalisch	*musical*
wissenschaftlich	*scientific*
anstrengend	*exhausting, strenuous, tiring*

Higher (wissenschaftlich, anstrengend)

School Life — School Routine and Lessons

die Schule	*school*
der Alltag	*daily routine, everyday life*
spät	*late*
früh	*early*
pünktlich	*punctual, in/on time, prompt*
anfangen	*to start*
enden	*to end, finish*
die Stunde	*lesson, period (school timetable)*

die Ferien	*holidays, school break*
der / die Schüler(in)	*pupil, school student*
der / die Student(in)	*student*
der / die Lehrer(in)	*teacher*
der / die Direktor(in)	*headteacher, principal*
der Unterricht	*lessons, classes, teaching, tuition*
die Klasse	*class*
das Klassenzimmer	*classroom*
lernen	*to learn, study*
erklären	*to explain*
lesen	*to read*
schreiben	*to write*
wiederholen	*to repeat*
übersetzen	*to translate*
teilen	*to divide*
die Hausaufgaben	*homework*
die Aufgabe	*task, exercise, assignment*
die Aktivität	*activity*
die Tätigkeit	*activity*
die Rechnung	*calculation*
der Kurs	*course*
das Papier	*paper*
das Blatt	*sheet*
die Grundschule (H)	*primary school*
das Gymnasium (H)	*grammar school*

Higher:

die Übung	*practice, exercise*
unterrichten	*to teach, tutor*
die Erklärung	*explanation*
der Satz	*sentence, phrase*
bitten um	*to request (+ noun), ask for (+ noun)*

School Life — During Break

die Pause	*break, pause*
der Club	*club*
die Mannschaft	*team*
der Sportplatz	*sports pitch*
die Kantine	*canteen, cafeteria*
die Information	*information*
der / die Trainer(in)	*coach*
reden	*to talk*
spielen	*to play*
dauern	*to last, take (time)*

Higher:

die Turnhalle	*gymnasium*
die Sportanlage	*sports facility*
die Anlage	*facility, complex*

School Pressures and Difficulties

die Ausbildung	*training, education, development*
die Regel	*rule*
streng	*strict, severe*
sollen	*to ought to, be supposed to, should*

müssen	*to have to, must*
dürfen	*to be allowed to, may*
nötig	*necessary, required*
erlauben	*to allow, permit*
verboten	*forbidden, banned*
die Uniform	*uniform*
das Mobbing	*bullying*
erfolgreich	*successful*
der Erfolg	*success*
das Studium	*study, studies*
sich vorbereiten (auf)	*to prepare oneself (for)*
die Prüfung	*exam(ination), test*
die Klassenarbeit	*school test*
die Antwort	*answer, reply, response*
antworten (auf)	*to answer, respond, reply*
beantworten	*to answer*
das Zeugnis	*report*
das Schulzeugnis	*school report*
die Note	*mark, grade*
die Leistung	*performance, achievement*
erreichen	*to achieve, reach*
sitzen bleiben / sitzenbleiben	*to repeat a school year*
richtig	*right, correct*
falsch	*false, wrong*
der Fehler	*mistake, error*

stimmen	*to be correct*
verbessern	*to improve, correct*
verstehen	*to understand*
üben	*to practise*
die Unterstützung	*support*
unterstützen	*to support*
hilfsbereit	*helpful, cooperative*
die Hilfe	*help, assistance*
fragen (nach)	*to ask (about)*
sich fragen	*to wonder*
die Arbeit	*work*
arbeiten (an [dat.])	*to work (on)*
der / die Jugendliche	*(the) young person, adolescent*
ein Jugendlicher / eine Jugendliche	*(a) young person, adolescent*
Jugendliche	*young people*
die Jugendlichen	*(the) young people*
jung	*young*
die Erfahrung	*experience*
das Interesse	*interest*

Higher

die Bildung	*education, learning*
bilden	*to educate*
verbieten	*to forbid, prohibit, ban*
die Herausforderung	*challenge*
das Abitur	*school leaving exams, A levels*

Higher

untersuchen	*to examine, research*
prüfen	*to examine, check*
der Versuch	*attempt, experiment*
abgeben	*to give in, hand in, submit*
das Ergebnis	*result, outcome*
erhalten	*to receive*
die Fähigkeit	*ability, capability, skill*
die Kenntnis	*knowledge*
der Druck	*pressure, stress*
bestehen	*to pass (an exam)*
leisten	*to perform, achieve, do*

Higher

aufpassen	*to pay attention, take care*
konzentrieren (auf)	*to concentrate (on)*
sich konzentrieren (auf)	*to concentrate (on)*
die Entwicklung	*development*
die Verantwortung	*responsibility*
die Diskussion	*discussion, debate*
der Austausch	*exchange, replacement*
erfahren	*to experience, find out*

Sentence Builder — Your School

You may be too cool for school, but nothing's cooler than a fresh German sentence...

Use the sentence builder to answer this question: **'Wie ist deine Schule?'**

Example: In meiner Schule haben wir einen Sportplatz und viele Clubs. Mir gefallen die Stunden, denn ich kann neue Informationen lernen. Ein Nachteil ist, dass die Prüfungen schwierig sind, aber ich verstehe den Grund dafür.

In meiner Schule *In my school*	gibt es *there is*	einen Sportplatz *a sports pitch*	und *and*	hilfsbereite Lehrer. *helpful teachers.*
Higher: In meinem Gymnasium *In my grammar school*	haben wir *we have*	eine Kantine *a canteen*		viele Clubs. *lots of clubs.*
		H: eine Turnhalle *a gymnasium*		moderne Klassenzimmer. *modern classrooms.*

Ich mag *I like*	die Stunden, *the lessons*	denn *because*	ich kann neue Informationen lernen. *I can learn new information.*
Ich liebe *I love*	die Aktivitäten, *the activities*		ich kann meine Leistung verbessern. *I can improve my performance.*
Mir gefallen *I like*	die Aufgaben, *the assignments*		sie helfen mir beim Lernen. *they help me with my learning.*

Ein Nachteil *A disadvantage*	ist, dass *is that*	die Uniform sehr unbequem ist, *the uniform is very uncomfortable,*	und ich finde das ärgerlich. *and I find that annoying.*
Ein negativer Aspekt *A negative aspect*		die Regeln streng sind, *the rules are strict,*	aber ich verstehe den Grund dafür. *but I understand the reason for it.*
		die Prüfungen schwierig sind, *the exams are difficult,*	

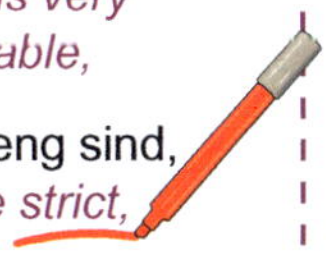

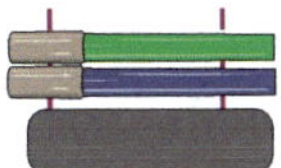

Time to hit the books — just not too hard, they're fragile...

If you want to go the extra mile, have a go at using the past tense for what your school used to be like, or the phrase 'ich möchte' to say what you'd like to change.

Future Study and Work

Education Post-16

die Ausbildung	*training, education, development*
die Universität, die Uni	*university*
das Studium	*study, studies*
der / die Student(in)	*student*
der Kurs	*course*
studieren	*to study (at university)*
lernen	*to learn, study*
die Note	*mark, grade*
verlassen	*to leave*
entscheiden	*to decide*
sich entscheiden (für)	*to decide (on)*
wählen	*to choose, select*
die Wahl	*choice, selection*
die Chance	*chance, opportunity*
die Möglichkeit	*possibility, chance, opportunity*
praktisch	*practical, useful*
träumen	*to dream*
H: die Oberstufe	*sixth form*
H: das Abitur	*school leaving exam, A levels*

Higher:

der Abschluss	*school leaving certificate, degree, diploma*
die Lehre	*apprenticeship*
die Gelegenheit	*opportunity, chance*

Career Choices and Ambitions

arbeiten	*to work*
die Arbeit	*work, job, employment*
der Job	*job*
der Beruf	*occupation, job, profession*
die Stelle	*job, position*
die Rolle	*role*
die Karriere	*career*
arbeitslos	*unemployed*
der / die Verkäufer(in)	*shop assistant, sales person*
der Arzt / die Ärztin	*doctor*
der / die Trainer(in)	*coach*
der / die Betreuer(in)	*carer, care worker*
der / die Polizist(in)	*police officer*
der / die Journalist(in)	*journalist*
der / die Direktor(in)	*director (of a company)*
der / die Sänger(in)	*singer*

der / die Schauspieler(in)	*actor*
der / die Künstler(in)	*artist, performer*
der Traum	*dream*
die Zukunft	*future*
das Ziel	*goal, aim, target*
suchen	*to look for*
der / die Chef(in)	*boss*
der Kollege / die Kollegin	*colleague*
der / die Mitarbeiter(in)	*employee, co-worker, colleague*
der Kunde / die Kundin	*customer, client*
der Arbeitsplatz	*workplace, job, employment*
das Büro	*office*
das Geschäft	*business, shop*
die Firma	*firm, company, business*
die Firmen	*firms, companies, businesses*
die Erfahrung	*experience*
die Aufgabe	*job, duty, task*
verdienen	*to earn*

Higher

die Arbeitslosigkeit	*unemployment*
der Bauer / die Bäuerin	*farmer*
der / die Wissenschaftler(in)	*scientist*
der Anwalt / die Anwältin	*lawyer, solicitor*

Higher

der / die Arbeitgeber(in)	*employer*
der / die Arbeitnehmer(in)	*employee, worker*
beschäftigen	*to employ*
die Industrie	*industry*
das Unternehmen	*company, firm*
die Organisation	*organisation*
die Gesellschaft	*company*
die Fabrik	*factory*
das Werk	*work, plant, factory*
die Maschine	*machine*
das Vorstellungsgespräch	*job interview*
die Zusammenarbeit	*cooperation, teamwork*
die Entwicklung	*development*
die Tätigkeit	*work, occupation*
der Lohn	*wage, pay, salary*
das Gehalt	*salary, pay, wages, earnings*
sich beschäftigen (mit)	*to be busy (with)*
besitzen	*to own*
gelingen	*to succeed*
schaffen	*to accomplish*
handeln	*to deal, trade*
vorhaben	*to be planning, have in mind, intend*

Sentence Builder — Your Future

By the time you reach the bottom of this page, you'll be in the future — no peeking...

Try answering this question: **'Was möchtest du in der Zukunft machen?'**

Example: In der Zukunft möchte ich Chemie an der Universität studieren. Dann will ich eine Ausbildung zum Arzt machen, weil ich gern Menschen helfe. Also werde ich Arbeitserfahrung suchen, die mir hilft, mich mehr in diesem Beruf zu entwickeln.

In der Zukunft *In the future,*	möchte ich *I would like*	Chemie an der Universität studieren. *to study chemistry at university.*
Nächstes Jahr *Next year,*	(H) würde ich gern *I would like*	ins Ausland reisen. *to travel abroad.*
Nach meinen Prüfungen *After my exams,*		(Higher) die Möglichkeit haben, einen Abschluss zu machen. *to have the chance to do a degree.*

Dann will ich *Then I want*	eine Ausbildung zum Arzt / zur Ärztin machen, *to do training to be a doctor*	weil *because*	ich gern Menschen helfe. *I like helping people.*
	als Betreuer(in) arbeiten, *to work as a carer*		ich gern mit anderen zusammenarbeite. *I like working with others.*
	eine Karriere als Lehrer(in) haben, *to have a career as a teacher*		(Higher) ich mich gern mit Arbeit beschäftige. *I like to be busy with work.*

(Higher)

Also *So,*	werde ich *I will*	Arbeitserfahrung suchen, *look for work experience*	die mir hilft, *that helps me*	mich mehr in diesem Beruf zu entwickeln. *to develop more in this profession.*
Um diesen Traum zu erreichen, *To achieve this dream,*		eine Gelegenheit finden, *find an opportunity*		in dieser Rolle viel zu schaffen. *to accomplish a lot in this role.*

Aaand welcome to the future! Although now it's the present...

Funny how that always seems to happen. Now try answering the question again, but this time use 'ich wollte' to say what you wanted to be when you were younger.

Free-time Activities

Cinema and TV

der Film	*film, movie*
das Kino	*cinema, movies, pictures*
das Ticket	*ticket*
die Karte	*ticket*
der Krimi	*thriller, detective film, crime film*
die Komödie	*comedy*
der Liebesfilm	*romantic film*
spannend	*exciting, thrilling*
aufregend	*exciting, thrilling*
streamen	*to stream*
sehen	*to watch, see*
ansehen	*to watch, look at*
sich [dat.] ansehen	*to watch, look at*
das Fernsehen	*television*
fernsehen	*to watch television*
die Sendung	*programme*
das Programm	*(TV) channel*
die Nachrichten	*the news*
die Seifenoper	*soap opera / series*

Higher

anschauen	*to watch, look at*
gucken, kucken	*to watch, look*
der Inhalt	*content, plot*

Higher

die Werbung	*advert, advertisement*
die Spannung	*suspense, tension*
die Serie	*series*
die Folge	*(TV) episode*
darstellen	*to depict, portray, show, represent*

Music

die Musik	*music*
die Note	*(musical) note*
singen	*to sing*
das Lied	*song*
hören	*to listen*
herunterladen	*to download*
der Rock	*rock music*
klassisch	*classical*
musikalisch	*musical*
die Band	*band, group*
die Gruppe	*group, band*
spielen	*to play*
lernen	*to learn, study*
das Instrument	*instrument*
das Konzert	*concert*

H

klingen	*to sound*
leise	*quiet, soft, quietly*

Sport

der Sport	*sport*
sportlich	*sporty, athletic*
aktiv	*active, energetic*
die Bewegung	*movement, motion, exercise*
die Fitness	*fitness*
das Fitness-Studio	*gym*
die Mannschaft	*team*
das Team	*team*
der Club	*club*
der Verein	*association, club, society*
das Training	*training*
der Platz	*(sport) pitch*
der / die Trainer(in)	*trainer*
der / die Spieler(in)	*player*
die Technik	*technique*
der Ball	*ball*
der Fußball	*football, soccer*
das Tor	*goal*
der Basketball	*basketball*
das Tennis	*tennis*
das Fahrrad	*bicycle*
Sport treiben	*to do sport*
treiben	*to drive, pursue*
üben	*to practise*
schlagen	*to hit, beat*
werfen	*to throw*
spazieren	*to go for a walk, stroll*
wandern	*to go on a walk / hike*
schwimmen	*to swim*
tauchen	*to dive*
joggen	*to jog*
springen	*to jump*
tanzen	*to dance*
laufen	*to run, walk*
der Lauf	*run, race*
die Runde	*round, lap*
der Wettbewerb	*competition, contest*
das Spiel	*game, match*
gewinnen	*to win*
verlieren	*to lose*
der / die Teilnehmer(in)	*participant, entrant*
teilnehmen (an [+ dat.])	*to take part (in)*

Higher

der / die Gegner(in)	*opponent, competitor, rival*
schießen (auf)	*to shoot (at), kick (ball)*
klettern	*to climb*

Going Out

ausgehen	*to go out*
treffen	*to meet*
sich treffen	*to meet up, get together*
einkaufen	*to shop*
kaufen	*to buy*
ausgeben	*to spend (money)*
kosten	*to cost*
die Kosten	*costs, expenses*
Lust auf (+ noun) haben	*to feel like (+ noun)*
das Geschäft	*business, shop*
der Besuch	*visit*
besuchen	*to visit*
das Restaurant	*restaurant*
die Speisekarte, die Karte	*menu*
die Rechnung	*bill*
das Museum	*museum*

Higher

das Gericht	*dish*
das Getränk	*drink*
schmecken	*to taste*
probieren	*to try, sample*
die Ausstellung	*exhibition, show*
die Museen	*museums*

Art and Theatre

die Kunst	*art*
das Bild	*picture, photo*
das Foto	*photo, photograph*
die Kultur	*culture*
das Theater	*theatre, drama*
das Stück	*play (theatre)*
die Rolle	*role, part*
interessieren	*to interest*
kreativ	*creative, creatively*
sich interessieren für	*to be interested in*
gefallen	*to please*

Higher

die Veranstaltung	*event, performance*
der Charakter	*character*
die Bühne	*stage*
malen	*to paint*
zeichnen	*to draw*

Other Activities

die Freizeit	*spare time, free time, leisure time*
die Ferien	*holidays, school break*
frei	*free, available*
lesen	*to read*
die Literatur	*literature*

der Roman	*novel*
das Buch	*book*
der Text	*text*
der Krimi	*thriller, detective story, crime story*
die Geschichte	*story*
der / die Autor(in)	*author, writer*
die Zeitung	*newspaper*
der Artikel	*article*
die Nachricht	*news, message*
das Videospiel	*video game*
der Computer	*computer*
der Spaß	*fun, joke*
die Party	*party*
kochen	*to cook*

der Brief	*letter*
schreiben (an)	*to write (to)*
die Aktivität	*activity*
freiwillig	*voluntary, voluntarily*
eigen	*own, private*

Higher

sich entspannen	*to relax, chill out*
amüsieren	*to enjoy*
sich amüsieren	*to enjoy oneself, have a good time*
unterhalten	*to entertain*
sich unterhalten	*to amuse oneself, chat*
sich melden	*to volunteer, enlist*

Sentence Builder — Your Hobbies

Revising your free time — ironic. Having duck-herding as a hobby — iconic.

Have a go at answering this question: **'Was machst du gern in deiner Freizeit?'**

Example: In meiner Freizeit schreibe ich Geschichten, weil es Spaß macht. Früher habe ich gern Sport getrieben und Filme im Kino gesehen. Wenn ich mehr Zeit hätte, würde ich im Sportzentrum klettern, um etwas Neues auszuprobieren.

In meiner Freizeit *In my free time,*	mache ich Kunst, *I do art*	weil *because*	es Spaß macht. *it is fun.*
Nach der Schule *After school,*	schreibe ich Geschichten, *I write stories*		es mich glücklich macht. *it makes me happy.*
H Um mich zu entspannen, *To relax,*	nehme ich an einem Fotoclub teil, *I take part in a photography club*		ich mich für kreative Aktivitäten interessiere. *I'm interested in creative activities.*

Früher habe ich gern *I used to like*	Videospiele gespielt *playing video games*	und *and*	in einer Gruppe gesungen. *singing in a group.*
Als Kind habe ich gern *As a child, I liked*	Sport getrieben *doing sport*		Filme im Kino gesehen. *watching films in the cinema.*
	Krimis gelesen *reading detective stories*		

Higher

Wenn ich mehr Zeit hätte, *If I had more time,*	würde ich *I would*	im Sportzentrum klettern *climb in the sports centre*	um mehr Leute kennenzulernen. *to meet more people.*
Wenn ich mehr Geld hätte, *If I had more money,*		auf der Bühne auftreten *perform on stage*	um mich zu amüsieren. *to have a good time.*
			um etwas Neues auszuprobieren. *to try out something new.*

Babies are great at basketball — they're always dribbling...

Now have a crack at writing about what activities your family and friends like to do.

Customs, Festivals and Celebrations

Celebrations

die Feier	*celebration, party, ceremony*
die Party	*party*
feiern	*to celebrate, party*
der Geburtstag	*birthday*
Herzlichen Glückwunsch	*Congratulations*
Herzlichen Glückwunsch zum Geburtstag	*Happy Birthday*
die Hochzeit	*wedding, marriage*
Silvester (m / n)	*New Year's Eve*
das Geschenk	*gift, present*
geben	*to give*
die Karte	*card*
heiraten	*to marry*
einladen	*to invite*
überraschen	*to surprise*
wünschen	*to want, wish, desire*
sich freuen auf	*to look forward to*

Higher

schenken	*to give (as a present)*
das Feuerwerk	*fireworks*
das Feuer	*fire, bonfire*
die Freude	*joy, pleasure*
amüsieren	*to amuse*
sich amüsieren	*to have a good time, enjoy (oneself)*

Customs and Festivals

das Weihnachten	*Christmas*
die Weihnachten	*Christmases*
der Heilige Abend	*Christmas Eve*
der erste Weihnachtstag	*Christmas Day*
das Lied	*song*
bekommen	*to get, receive*
Ostern (n)	*Easter*
die Kultur	*culture*
die Küche	*cuisine*
die Tradition	*tradition*
traditionell	*traditional, traditionally*
kulturell	*cultural*
historisch	*historical*
national	*national*
die Region	*region, area*
besondere	*special*
bunt	*colourful, colourfully*
gemeinsam	*common, in common, mutual, joint*
erleben	*to experience*
passieren	*to take place, happen, occur*
das Glück	*luck, good luck, fortune, happiness*
Deutsche	*Germans*
die Deutschen	*the Germans*

die Religion	*religion*
der Muslim	*Muslim (m)*
die Muslime	*Muslim (f)*
der Jude	*Jewish (m), Jewish person*
die Jüdin	*Jewish (f)*
der / die Christ(in)	*Christian*
der / die Hindu	*Hindu*
glauben (an)	*to believe (in), think*
das Fest	*festival, celebration*
Eid (al-Fitr) (n)	*Eid*
der Herr	*Lord (addressing God)*
der Himmel	*heaven*
das Licht	*light*
bekannt	*well-known, famous*
stattfinden	*to take place, occur*

Higher

hängen	*to hang*
der König	*king*
der Karneval	*Carnival*
die Gesellschaft	*society*
das Ereignis	*event, occurrence*
die Stimmung	*mood, atmosphere*
der Lärm	*noise*
das Gericht	*dish*
speziell	*special*
verbinden, sich verbinden	*to connect, link, unite*

Sentence Builder — Festivals

Get your party hat on, because it's time to talk about festivals you love to celebrate...

Answer this question: **'Wie feierst du dein Lieblingsfest?'**

Example: Jedes Jahr feiere ich Weihnachten mit meiner Familie. Normalerweise geben wir Geschenke und kochen traditionelles Essen. Als ich jünger war, habe ich am liebsten viel Süßes gegessen.

Jedes Jahr feiere ich *Every year I celebrate*	Weihnachten *Christmas*	mit *with*	meiner Familie. *my family.*
Manchmal feiere ich *Sometimes I celebrate*	Ostern *Easter*	bei *at the house of*	meinen Eltern. *my parents.*
	Eid *Eid*		meinen Freunden. *my friends.*
			meinen Großeltern. *my grandparents.*

Normalerweise *Normally*	hören wir Musik *we listen to music*	und *and*	nehmen an kulturellen Traditionen teil. *take part in cultural traditions.*
Oft *Often*	gehen wir in die Kirche / Moschee *we go to church / the mosque*		kochen traditionelles Essen. *cook traditional food.*
	geben wir Geschenke *we give gifts*		amüsieren uns zusammen. *enjoy ourselves together.*

Higher

Als Kind *As a child*	habe ich *I*	am liebsten viel Süßes gegessen. *liked eating lots of sweet things the most.*
Als ich jünger war, *When I was younger*		am meisten die aufregende Stimmung genossen. *enjoyed the exciting atmosphere most.*
Früher *In the past*		am liebsten spezielle Gerichte probiert. *liked trying special dishes best.*

I'll go get my wellies — oh, not that kind of festival...

Next, try talking about what you'll get up to for a festival next year — how exciting...

Celebrity Culture

Favourite Celebrities

der Star	celebrity, headliner
die Persönlichkeit	personality, celebrity
Lieblings- (+ noun)	favourite (+ noun)
der / die Sänger(in)	singer
die Gruppe	group, band
der / die Schauspieler(in)	actor
der / die Spieler(in)	player
der / die Autor(in)	author, writer
der / die Künstler(in)	artist, performer
die Band	band, group (music)
berühmt	famous
bekannt	well-known, famous
folgen	to follow
das Stück	play (theatre)
Haupt- (+ noun)	main (+ noun)
die Rolle	role, part
der Roman	novel
das Konzert	concert
die Musik	music
die Stimme	voice
das Video	video
das Foto	photo, photograph

das Fernsehen	television
die Sendung	programme
die Mannschaft	team
der Sport	sport
der Wunsch	wish, desire
aufregend	exciting, thrilling
kreativ	creative, creatively
wichtig	important
schön	lovely, beautiful
empfehlen	to recommend
singen	to sing
hören	to hear, listen
ansehen	to look at, watch

Higher

das Vorbild	role model, example
die Vorstellung	performance, imagination
die Veranstaltung	event, performance
der Eindruck	impression, effect
der Einfluss	influence
der Charakter	character
die Szene	scene
die Bühne	stage
die Serie	series
die Mode	fashion
unterhalten	to entertain

Higher

darstellen	*to depict, portray, show, represent*
auftreten	*to appear, occur, perform*

Celebrity Life

die Karriere	*career*
die Medien (pl)	*media*
die Zeitung	*newspaper*
das Interview	*interview*
das Bild	*picture, image, photo*
tragen	*to wear*
positiv	*positive*
negativ	*negative*
der Vorteil	*advantage, benefit*
der Nachteil	*disadvantage*
das Geld	*money, cash*
der Erfolg	*success*
der Preis	*prize, award*
der Fan	*fan, supporter*

der / die Zuschauer(in)	*viewer, spectator*
das Publikum	*audience, public*
beliebt	*popular*
reich	*rich, wealthy, abundant*
verdienen	*to earn, deserve*
scharfe Worte	*sharp words*
sich verhalten	*to behave, act*
öffentlich	*public*
normal	*normal*

Higher

die Wirklichkeit	*reality, truth*
die Rede	*speech, talk*
berichten	*to report*
das Gute	*the good thing*
die Reichen	*the rich (ones)*
wert	*worth, worthy of*
die Kritik	*criticism, review*
kritisieren	*to criticise*
die Öffentlichkeit	*public*
das Opfer	*sacrifice, victim, casualty*
anschauen	*to look at, watch*
beobachten	*to observe, watch*
sinnvoll	*sensible, wise*

Sentence Builder — Celebrities

You'll play the starring role in your exam, so better get rehearsing those lines...

Give this question a try: **'Wer ist dein Lieblingsstar? Warum?'**

Example: Mein Lieblingsstar ist eine Sängerin, die sehr berühmt ist.
Ich mag sie, weil sie nett zu den Fans ist und interessante Interviews gibt.
Man hält sie für ein positives Vorbild, da sie Opfern von Online-Mobbing hilft.

Mein Lieblingsstar *My favourite celebrity* Meine Lieblingspersönlichkeit *My favourite personality*	ist *is*	ein Schauspieler / eine Schauspielerin *an actor* ein Sänger / eine Sängerin *a singer* ein Autor / eine Autorin *an author*	der / die *who*	sehr berühmt ist. *is very famous.* viele Preise gewinnt. *wins many prizes.* erfolgreich ist. *is successful.*

Ich mag ihn / sie, *I like him / her* Ich folge ihm / ihr, *I follow him / her*	weil er / sie *because he / she*	nett zu den Fans ist *is nice to fans* **H** sich gut in der Öffentlichkeit verhält *acts well in public*	und *and*	kreativ ist. *is creative.* hart arbeitet. *works hard.* interessante Interviews gibt. *gives interesting interviews.*

Higher

Man hält ihn / sie für *He / she is thought of as*	ein positives Vorbild, *a positive role model* einen guten Einfluss, *a good influence*	da er / sie *because he / she*	den Armen Geld gibt. *gives money to the poor.* Opfern von Online-Mobbing hilft. *helps victims of online bullying.* gut bei wichtigen Veranstaltungen spricht. *speaks well at important events.*

I saw the fruit bowl glowing — must be the limelight...

To practise talking about the pros and cons of fame, have a go at writing a few sentences that describe both the good and bad things about being a celebrity.

Travel and Tourism

Where to Go

das Land	*country, land, state, countryside*
die Welt	*world*
die Region	*region, area*
Deutschland (n)	*Germany*
die Bundesrepublik, BRD	*Federal Republic (of Germany)*
Österreich (n)	*Austria*
das Bundesland	*state, province (Germany, Austria)*
die Schweiz	*Switzerland*
die Türkei	*Turkey*
Großbritannien (n)	*Great Britain*
England (n)	*England*
Frankreich (n)	*France*
Italien (n)	*Italy*
Spanien (n)	*Spain*
Griechenland (n)	*Greece*
München	*Munich*
Köln	*Cologne*
Wien	*Vienna*
der Rhein	*the Rhine*
die Ostsee	*the Baltic Sea*
Europa (n)	*Europe*
die EU (Europäische Union)	*EU (European Union)*
das Ausland	*abroad, foreign countries*
die Temperatur	*temperature*
die Sonne	*sun*
sonnig	*sunny*
heiß	*hot*
warm	*warm*
kalt	*cold*
der Urlaub	*holiday*
der Besuch	*visit*
fremd	*foreign*
fahren	*to go (by transport), drive*
reisen	*to travel*
besuchen	*to visit*
planen	*to plan*

Higher

Amerika (n)	*America*
die USA (Vereinigte Staaten von Amerika)	*USA (United States of America)*
international	*international*
das Klima	*climate*
gelten	*to be valid*

Accommodation

das Hotel	*hotel*
die Wohnung	*apartment, flat*
das Zimmer	*room*
der Raum	*room, space*
der Platz	*place, room, square, seat*
das Bett	*bed*
der Gast	*guest, visitor (m)*
die Gästin	*guest, visitor (f)*
der / die Besucher(in)	*visitor, guest*
die Nähe	*vicinity, proximity*
bleiben	*to stay, remain*
wohnen	*to stay (holidays)*
schlafen	*to sleep*
organisieren	*to organise*
teuer	*expensive, dear, costly*
günstig	*cheap, favourable, good, cheaply*
billig	*cheap, cheaply*
sauber	*clean*
schmutzig	*dirty, filthy*
bequem	*comfortable*
voll	*full*
frei	*free, available*
die Landschaft	*landscape, countryside*
die Insel	*island*
die Küste	*coast, shore*
das Meer	*sea, ocean*
der Berg	*mountain, hill*
der Wald	*forest, wood*
der Blick	*view, look, glance*
willkommen	*welcome*
H der Aufenthalt	*stay, residence*
H das Zelt	*tent*

Travel

der Verkehr	*transport, traffic*
das Mittel	*means*
nehmen	*to take*
das Auto	*car*
das Fahrrad	*bicycle*
der Bus	*bus*
die Busse (pl)	*buses*
der Zug	*train*
die Bahn	*train, railway*
der Bahnhof	*(railway) station*
das Schiff	*ship*
das Flugzeug	*aeroplane, plane, aircraft*
der Flughafen	*airport*
fliegen	*to fly*
die Karte	*ticket, card*
das Ticket	*ticket*
die Reise	*journey, trip, voyage*
die Fahrt	*drive, trip*
der / die Fahrer(in)	*driver*
das Ziel	*destination*

der Kilometer	*kilometre*
die Linie	*line, route (e.g. bus)*
kommen	*to come*
mitnehmen	*to take along*
ankommen (in [dat.])	*to arrive (at)*
verlassen	*to leave*
zurückkommen	*to return*
warten (auf)	*to wait (for)*
pünktlich	*in/on time, punctual, prompt*
spät	*late*
weg	*gone, vanished, away*
unterwegs	*on the way*
direkt	*direct, straight, directly, immediately*
vorne, vorn	*at/to the front, ahead*
weiter	*further*
zurück	*back*

Higher

die Straßenbahn	*tram*
die U-Bahn	*metro, underground railway*
das Boot	*boat*
der Flug	*flight*
die Verbindung	*connection, link*
die Geschwindigkeit	*speed*
ziehen	*to move*

What to Do

der Ort	*place, town, location*
das Gebäude	*building*
die Gebäude	*buildings*
das Museum	*museum*
das Schloss	*castle*
der Markt	*market*
der Strand	*beach, shore*
der See	*lake*
die See	*sea*
die Quelle	*spring*
das Restaurant	*restaurant*
das Café	*café, coffee shop*
historisch	*historical*
bekannt	*well-known, famous*
berühmt	*famous*
der Plan	*plan*
die Kultur	*culture*
kulturell	*cultural*
die Küche	*cuisine*
der / die Tourist(in)	*tourist*
nehmen	*to have something to eat or drink*
verbringen	*to spend (time)*
erleben	*to experience*
die Erfahrung	*experience*
finden	*to find*
sich finden	*to be found, find oneself*

bestellen	*to reserve, order*
entspannend	*relaxing*
ruhig	*quiet, calm*
das Geld	*money, cash*
der Euro	*euro (unit of currency)*
kosten	*to cost*
ausgeben	*to spend (money)*
zahlen	*to pay*
die Kamera	*camera*
das Foto	*photo, photograph*
die Sprache	*language, speech*

Higher

die Hauptstadt	*capital city*
sich entspannen	*to relax, chill out*
entdecken	*to discover*
erfahren	*to experience, find out*
führen	*to lead, guide*
unterhalten	*to entertain*
anbieten	*to offer, serve something (with sth.)*
der Ausflug	*excursion, trip, outing*

Sentence Builder — Your Holidays

Everyone loves a holiday, and with these sentences you'll be jetting off in no time...

Answer this question: **'Was machst du normalerweise in den Ferien?'**

Example: Jedes Jahr fahren wir gern auf eine Insel, weil es sonnig ist. Ich fahre lieber mit dem Zug und ich bleibe regelmäßig in einer bequemen Wohnung. Nächstes Jahr werde ich durch Italien reisen, um die historischen Gebäude zu sehen.

Normalerweise *Normally* In den Sommerferien *In the summer holidays* Jedes Jahr *Every year*	reise ich gern *I like travelling* fahren wir gern *we like going*	ins Ausland, *abroad* an die Küste, *to the coast* auf eine Insel, *to an island*	weil *because* H: wo *where*	es sonnig ist. *it is sunny.* die Landschaft schön ist. *the landscape is beautiful.*

Ich fahre gern *I like travelling* Ich fahre lieber *I prefer travelling*	mit dem Zug *by train* mit dem Flugzeug *by plane* mit dem Auto *by car* H: mit dem Boot *by boat*	und ich wohne oft *and I often stay* und ich bleibe regelmäßig *and I regularly stay*	in einem billigen Hotel. *in a cheap hotel.* in einer bequemen Wohnung. *in a comfortable apartment.* H: in einem großen Zelt. *in a big tent.*

Higher

Nächstes Jahr *Next year* Nächsten Sommer *Next summer*	werde ich *I will* würde meine Familie gern *my family would like to*	eine Hauptstadt in Europa besuchen, *visit a capital city in Europe* nach München fahren, *go to Munich* durch Italien reisen, *travel through Italy*	um *in order*	die historischen Gebäude zu sehen. *to see the historical buildings.* bekannte Museen zu besuchen. *to visit famous museums.*

Sun, sea and a sentence builder — my perfect holiday...

Next, use the perfect tense to describe a holiday you had when you were younger.

Media and Technology

Technology

die Technologie	*technology*
die Technik	*technology*
das System	*system*
das Programm	*program*
der Computer	*computer*
die Kamera	*camera*
der / das Laptop	*laptop*
das Handy	*mobile phone*
das Telefon	*telephone*
die SMS	*text message*
die / das App	*app*
der Ton	*sound, tone*
anrufen	*to phone, ring*
simsen	*to text*
schicken	*to send*
funktionieren	*to function, work*
digital	*digital, digitally*
modern	*modern, up-to-date*
kompliziert	*complicated, complex*
nützlich	*useful*
schnell	*quickly, fast*
kaputt	*broken, ruined*
neu	*new, recent*
teuer	*expensive, dear, costly*
einfach	*simple, easy*

Higher

das Gerät	*appliance, tool*
telefonieren	*to (make a telephone) call*
aufladen	*to charge*
klingen	*to sound, ring*
sich [dat.] vorstellen	*to imagine*
technisch	*technical*
speziell	*specific*

The Internet

das Internet	*internet*
die (Web)Seite	*(web) page*
das WLAN	*Wi-Fi®*
die / das E-Mail	*e-mail*
die Kommunikation	*communication*
der Kontakt	*contact*
die Nachricht	*news, message*
online	*online*
streamen	*to stream*
einkaufen	*to shop*
sich [dat.] ansehen	*to look at, watch*
planen	*to plan, design*
die Sicherheit	*security, safety*
der Schutz	*protection*
die Information	*information*
die Quelle	*source*
das Wort	*word*
sicher	*safe, secure*
fremd	*strange*

Higher

das Netz	*net, network, web*
die Verbindung	*connection, link*
verbinden	*to connect, link*
der / die Leser(in)	*reader*
sich informieren (über + noun)	*to find out (about + noun)*
informieren	*to inform*
die Studie	*study, survey*
die Werbung	*advertising, advert(isement)*
die Daten	*data*
das Opfer	*victim, sacrifice, casualty*
verstecken	*to hide*
stehlen	*to steal*

Social Media

Medien	*media*
soziale Medien	*social media*
der / die Influencer(in)	*influencer*
das Video	*video*
das / der Blog	*blog*
der Post	*(blog) post*
das Gespräch	*conversation, talk*
hochladen	*to upload*
herunterladen	*to download*
teilen	*to share*
folgen	*to follow*
die Gefahr	*danger, risk, threat*
das Risiko	*risk, hazard, danger*
das Mobbing	*bullying*
privat	*private, personal*
persönlich	*personal*
echt	*genuine, real, genuinely, really*

Higher

aufnehmen	*to record*
drehen	*to film, turn*
reagieren (auf)	*to react (to)*
die Risiken	*risks, hazards, dangers*
vorsichtig	*cautious, careful, wary*

Sentence Builder — Technology

Hungry for some more sentence-building practice? Take a megabyte out of this page...

Have a go at answering this question: **'Was denkst du über Technologie?'**

Example: Ich denke, dass das Internet nützlich ist, denn man kann Informationen einfach teilen. Jeden Tag benutze ich meinen Laptop und ich sehe lustige Videos. Aber moderne Technik hat Nachteile, weil es oft Online-Mobbing gibt.

Ich denke, dass *I think that* Ich glaube, dass *I believe that* [Higher] Ich bin der Meinung, dass *I'm of the opinion that*	Technologie *technology* das Internet *the internet*	nützlich ist, *is useful* wunderbar ist, *is wonderful* toll ist, *is great*	denn *because*	man kann mit anderen in Kontakt bleiben. *you can stay in contact with others.* man kann Informationen einfach teilen. *you can share information easily.*

Jeden Tag *Every day* Persönlich *Personally* Ein paar Stunden pro Tag *A couple of hours per day*	benutze ich *I use* [H] verwende ich *I use*	mein Handy *my mobile phone* meinen Laptop *my laptop* Apps *apps* [H] das Netz *the web*	und ich schicke meinen Freunden Nachrichten. *and I send messages to my friends.* und ich sehe lustige Videos. *and I watch funny videos.* und ich lade Posts hoch. *and I upload blog posts.*

Aber moderne Technik *However, modern technology*	hat Nachteile, *has disadvantages* kann gefährlich sein, *can be dangerous* ist manchmal negativ, *is sometimes negative*	weil *because*	es oft Online-Mobbing gibt. *there is often online bullying.* [Higher] man deine Daten stehlen kann. *your data can be stolen.*

I follow some dolphins online — they do a great podcast...

It's just a lot of 'Eeee, Eeee!' but I like it. Anyway, if you want an extra challenge, have a go at using different tenses to write about technology in the past and future.

Where People Live

The Home

wohnen	*to live*
das Haus	*house*
die Wohnung	*apartment, flat*
der Raum	*room, space*
das Zimmer	*room*
das Wohnzimmer	*living room, lounge, sitting room*
die Küche	*kitchen*
das Badezimmer	*bathroom*
das Bad	*bath, bathroom, spa*
die Toilette	*toilet*
das Büro	*office*
der Keller	*cellar, basement*
der Gang	*corridor, hallway*
der Garten	*garden*
das Bett	*bed*
der Tisch	*table*
der Stuhl	*chair*
die Tür	*door*
das Fenster	*window*
die Wand	*wall*
der Boden	*floor, ground*
das Tor	*gate*
das Blatt	*leaf*
die Pflanze	*plant*
der / die Nachbar(in)	*neighbour*
groß	*big, great*
klein	*small, little*
hoch	*high, tall*
schön	*lovely, beautiful*
bequem	*comfortable*
ruhig	*quiet, calm*
laut	*loud, noisy*
sauber	*clean*
nutzlos	*useless*
die Ordnung	*order, tidiness*
die Ruhe	*silence, peace, rest*
nach Hause	*(to) home*
zu Hause	*at home*
der Müll	*rubbish, waste, litter*
aufstehen	*to get up*
sich anziehen	*to get dressed*
machen	*to do, make*
helfen	*to help*
kochen	*to cook, boil*
essen	*to eat*
sich kümmern um	*to take care of*
verlassen	*to leave*
schlafen	*to sleep*

Higher

der Haushalt	*household, budget*
der Schlüssel	*key*
das Dach	*roof*
der Hof	*yard*
die Mauer	*wall*

Higher

besitzen	*to own, have*
einschlafen	*to fall asleep, doze off*
angenehm	*pleasant*

The Local Area — Places

das Dorf	*village*
die Stadt	*town, city*
der Ort	*place, town, location*
die Region	*region, area*
die Gegend	*area, region*
das Gebiet	*region, area, territory*
das Zentrum	*centre, middle*
die Mitte	*middle, centre*
die Straße	*street, road*
die Hauptstraße	*main street*
die Umgebung	*surroundings, neighbourhood*
das Gebäude	*building*
die Gebäude	*buildings*
der Bahnhof	*railway station*
das Krankenhaus	*hospital*
die Polizei	*police*
der Supermarkt	*supermarket*
die Post	*post office, post, mail*
das Café	*café, coffee shop*
der Imbiss	*take away, diner, snack bar, snack, refreshment*
der Markt	*market*
die Kirche	*church*
die Moschee	*mosque*
die Synagoge	*synagogue*
der Tempel	*temple*
das Kino	*cinema*
das Theater	*theatre*
die Bank	*bank, bench*
der Park	*park*
das Feld	*field, pitch, court (sport)*
der Platz	*place, room, square, seat, pitch (sport)*
der Strand	*beach, shore*
der Wald	*forest, wood*
das Stadion	*stadium*
das Hotel	*hotel*
die Brücke	*bridge*
die Stelle	*place, position*
bauen	*to build, construct*
liegen	*to be situated*
fehlen	*to lack, be absent, be missing*
es gibt	*there is, there are*
es gab	*there was, there were, there used to be*

Higher

der Bereich	*area, region, district*
die Bevölkerung	*population, people, members of the public*
der / die Bürger(in)	*citizen*
der / die Bürgermeister(in)	*mayor*
der / die Einwohner(in)	*resident, inhabitant*
die Fabrik	*factory*
das Werk	*work, plant, factory*
die Industrie	*industry*
die Anlage	*facility, complex*
der Bau	*construction, building*
aufbauen	*to build up, construct*
existieren	*to exist*

The Local Area — Shopping

einkaufen	*to shop*
bezahlen	*to pay*
akzeptieren	*to accept*
ausgeben	*to spend (money)*
verkaufen	*to sell*
das Geschäft	*business, shop*
die Kleidung	*clothes, outfit*
das Hemd	*shirt*
das T-Shirt	*T-shirt*
die Jacke	*jacket*
die Hose (sing.)	*trousers*
der Rock	*skirt*
das Kleid	*dress*
der Schuh	*shoe*
Schuhe (m)	*shoes*
das Paar	*pair, couple*
die Tasche	*pocket, bag*
die Uhr	*clock, watch*
der Preis	*price*
die Rechnung	*bill, invoice*
der Kunde	*customer (m)*
die Kundin	*customer (f)*
passen	*to fit, suit*
tragen	*to carry, wear*
abholen	*to get, fetch, pick up*
öffnen	*to open*
schließen	*to close, shut*
offen	*open*
geschlossen	*closed, shut*

Higher

der Laden	*shop*
wechseln	*to change, exchange (money)*
liefern	*to deliver, supply*
sich [dat.] anziehen (+ noun)	*to put on (+ noun)*
hübsch	*pretty, cute, lovely*
hässlich	*ugly, hideous*

Directions and Weather

die Richtung	*direction, way*
der Weg	*path, way, method*
linke	*left (adj.)*
rechte	*right (adj.)*
links	*on / to the left*
rechts	*on / to the right*
hier	*here*
da	*there*
dort	*there*
weiter	*further, (carry) on*
oben	*upstairs, above, up there*
unten	*downstairs, below, down*
hinter	*behind*
hinten	*at / in the back*
neben	*next to, beside*
gegenüber	*opposite, across from*
weg	*gone, vanished, away*
die Nähe	*vicinity, proximity*
der Kilometer	*kilometre*
nahe, nah	*near(by), close*
weit	*far*
eng	*narrow, close, tight*
der Norden, Nord-	*north*
der Osten, Ost-	*east*
der Süden, Süd-	*south*
der Westen, West-	*west*

das Wetter	*weather*
die Temperatur	*temperature*
der / das Grad	*degree (temperature)*
regnen	*to rain*
schneien	*to snow*
sonnig	*sunny*
heiß	*hot*
warm	*warm*
kalt	*cold*
dunkel	*dark, gloomy*
die Sonne	*sun*
der Schnee	*snow*
der Wind	*wind*
der Himmel	*sky*
die Höhe	*height, altitude*
der Frühling	*spring*
der Sommer	*summer*
der Herbst	*autumn*
der Winter	*winter*

Higher

die Lage	*situation, location, position*
die Ecke	*corner*
der Rand	*edge*
fern	*far, distant*
entfernt	*distant, away*
drinnen	*inside, indoors*
heraus	*out, outside*
hinaus	*out, beyond*
das Klima	*climate*
der Stern	*star*
mir ist...	*I feel...*

Sentence Builder — Your Town

Go to town on this sentence builder and you'll come out with one fab answer.

Use the sentence builder to answer this question: **'Wie ist deine Stadt?'**

Example: Meine Stadt liegt neben einem Wald und ist historisch.
Es gibt einige Geschäfte, aber meiner Gegend fehlt ein Theater.
Ab und zu ist mir sehr kalt, aber normalerweise finde ich das Wetter schön.

Meine Stadt *My town / city*	ist *is*	in Ostengland *in the East of England*	und ist *and is*	klein. *small.*
Mein Dorf *My village*	liegt *is situated*	im Norden *in the North*		groß. *big.*
Mein Gebiet *My region*		nahe am Meer *near to the sea*		historisch. *historical.*
		neben einem Wald *next to a forest*		modern. *modern.*

Es gibt *There are*	viele *many*	Cafés, *cafés,*	aber meiner Gegend fehlt *but my area lacks*	ein Kino. *a cinema.*
	einige *some*	Plätze, *squares,*	aber meine Region braucht *but my area needs*	eine Post. *a post office.*
	H mehrere *several*	Geschäfte, *shops,*		ein Theater. *a theatre.*
				ein Stadion. *a stadium.*

Ab und zu *Now and then*	ist mir sehr kalt, *I feel very cold,*	aber meistens *but mostly*	ist die Temperatur warm. *the temperature is warm.*
Manchmal *Sometimes*	ist es wirklich dunkel, *it's really gloomy,*	aber normalerweise *but normally*	finde ich das Wetter schön. *I find the weather lovely.*
	regnet es den ganzen Tag, *it rains the whole day,*		H ist das Klima angenehm. *the climate is pleasant.*

Talking about my town? That's right up my street...

To boast about your local area even more (which I'm sure you'd love to do), say some sentences about what you did there last week and what the weather was like.

Environmental and Social Issues

Environmental Problems

die Umwelt	*environment*
die Natur	*nature*
die Erde	*earth, ground, soil, world*
die Welt	*world*
das Problem	*problem*
verschmutzen	*to pollute, contaminate*
zerstören	*to destroy, ruin*
schmutzig	*dirty, filthy*
der Müll	*litter, rubbish, waste*
werfen	*to throw*
weg	*away, gone, vanished*
wegwerfen	*to throw away*
die Menge	*quantity, amount, a lot of, crowd (people)*
das Fahrzeug	*vehicle*
natürlich	*natural, naturally*
draußen	*outside, outdoors*
überall	*everywhere*

Higher

das Klima	*climate*
der Faktor	*factor*
menschlich	*human (adj.)*
der Stoff	*material, substance, fabric*
brennen	*to burn*
produzieren	*to produce*
die Risiken	*risks, hazards, dangers*
riesig	*huge, great, tremendous, giant, massive, enormous*
erschrecken	*to frighten, be startled*
aktuell	*current, up-to-date, topical*
die Fabrik	*factory*

Environmental Impacts

die Konsequenz	*consequence*
die Sorge	*worry, care*
sorgen	*to worry, care*
die Temperatur	*temperature*
der / das Grad	*degree (temperature)*
steigen	*to increase, go up, climb*
verschwinden	*to disappear*
das Wetter	*weather*
die Luft	*air*
das Meer	*sea, ocean*
der Fluss	*river*
der Lauf	*course*
der Wald	*forest, wood*
der Baum	*tree*

die Pflanze	*plant*
der Himmel	*sky*
der Klimawandel	*climate change*
die Veränderung	*change*
der Zustand	*condition, state*
die Folge	*result, consequence*
der Effekt	*effect*
das Ereignis	*event, occurrence, incident*
die Ursache	*cause*
verursachen	*to cause*
das Feuer	*fire*
wachsen	*to grow, increase*
der / die Wissenschaftler(in)	*scientist*
warnen (vor [dat.])	*to warn (of / about)*

Higher (der Klimawandel – warnen)

Protecting the Environment — Actions

der Schutz	*protection, conservation*
schützen (vor [dat.])	*to protect (from)*
umweltfreundlich	*environmentally friendly*
das Recycling	*recycling*
recyceln	*to recycle*
sammeln	*to collect, gather*
verboten	*forbidden, banned*
öffentlich	*public*
der Verkehr	*traffic, transport*
das Mittel	*means*
das Ziel	*goal, aim, target*
sauber	*clean*
praktisch	*practical, useful*
die Lösung	*solution, answer*
lösen	*to solve, loosen*
die Verantwortung	*responsibility*
erhalten	*to preserve, maintain*
trennen	*to separate*
reduzieren	*to reduce, decrease*
verbieten	*to forbid, prohibit, ban*
sich [dat.] lassen	*to have sth done*
das Elektroauto	*electric car, electric vehicle*
vorsichtig	*cautious, careful, wary*
die Suche	*search*
die Methode	*method, technique*
die Gegenwart	*present*
künftig	*future, from now on*
langfristig	*long-term, in the long run*
rein	*pure, clear, clean, total(ly)*

Higher (die Lösung – rein)

Protecting the Environment — Energy Sources

grün	*green*
die Energie	*energy*
sparen	*to save*
die Quelle	*source*
das Licht	*light*
die Sonne	*sun*
der Wind	*wind*

Higher

die Kraft	*power*
der Haushalt	*household*
verwenden	*to use*
das Angebot	*offer, supply*
bieten	*to offer, provide*
das Gerät	*tool, appliance, piece of equipment*
das Projekt	*project*

Social Issues

die Schwierigkeit	*difficulty*
der Nachteil	*disadvantage*
der Vorteil	*advantage, benefit*
arbeitslos	*unemployed*
der Unterschied	*difference*
reich	*rich, wealthy, abundant*
arm	*poor*
die Kosten	*costs, expenses*
kosten	*to cost*
gleich	*equal*
frei	*free*
der Hunger	*hunger*
leiden (an [dat.])	*to suffer (from)*
leiden (unter [dat.])	*to suffer (as a result of)*
fehlen	*to lack, be missing*
der Krieg	*war*
die Gewalt	*violence, force*
die Gefahr	*danger, risk, threat*
gefährlich	*dangerous, risky*
die Situation	*situation*
treiben	*to drive*
brechen	*to break*
die Freiheit	*freedom*
das Recht	*right, law*
die Stimme	*vote*
die Wahl	*choice, election, selection*
die Mehrheit	*majority*
der Aspekt	*aspect*
stimmen (für)	*to vote (for)*
sich erklären	*to declare oneself*
wählen	*to choose, elect, vote, select*
die Leute (pl)	*people*
die Hilfe	*help, assistance*
freiwillig	*voluntary, voluntarily*
retten	*to save, rescue*
verbessern	*to improve*

fallen	*to fall, decrease*
abnehmen	*to decrease, reduce*
breit	*wide, broad*
weit	*far, wide, widely*

Higher

die Gesellschaft	*society*
die Wirtschaft	*economy, commerce*
die Arbeitslosigkeit	*unemployment*
sich [dat.] leisten	*to afford*
die Bedingung	*condition, stipulation, requirement*
die Krise	*crisis*
die Schuld	*guilt, blame, debt*
knapp	*scarce, slim*
der Kampf	*fight, struggle, battle*
kämpfen	*to fight, struggle, battle*
der Konflikt	*conflict, dispute*
der Schaden	*damage, harm*
der Flüchtling	*refugee*
das Opfer	*victim, casualty*
der Gegner	*enemy*
zwingen	*to force, compel*
verhalten	*to control*
die Tat	*deed, action*
stehlen	*to steal*

Higher

das Gesetz	*law*
gerecht	*just, fair*
die Einführung	*introduction*
gründen	*to establish, found*
feststellen	*to establish, detect, determine, realise*
die Bundesregierung	*federal government*
die Regierung	*rule, government*
das Volk	*people*
der / die Bürger(in)	*citizen*
der Fortschritt	*progress*
das Zeichen	*sign, symbol*
die Bildung	*education, learning, creation, formation*
bilden	*to educate, form*
melden	*to report, register*
sich (freiwillig) melden	*to volunteer, enlist*
erhöhen	*to raise, increase*
die Organisation	*organisation*
der Fall	*fall, case*
der Bericht	*report, record*
die Umfrage	*survey*

Higher

untersuchen	*to examine, investigate, research*
fordern	*to demand, claim*
drohen	*to threaten*
beweisen	*to prove, demonstrate*
aufnehmen	*to take in*

Higher

lassen	*to let, allow*
sich beschäftigen mit	*to deal with*
die Erinnerung	*memory, reminder*
sinnvoll	*sensible, meaningful*
verantwortlich	*responsible, in charge*

Sentence Builder — Environment

I do all I can to protect the environment — I just can't help it, it's in my nature.

Try answering this question: **'Wie kann man die Umwelt schützen?'**

Example: Man soll mehr recyceln, weil das beim Umweltschutz hilft. Im Alltag benutze ich immer öffentliche Verkehrsmittel, denn ich will umweltfreundlicher sein. Wenn die Leute die Umwelt weiter verschmutzen, werden die Temperaturen steigen.

Man soll *You ought to*	mehr recyceln, *recycle more,*	da es besser für die Umwelt ist. *as it's better for the environment.*
Man kann *You can*	weniger Energie zu Hause benutzen, *use less energy at home,*	weil das beim Umweltschutz hilft. *because that helps to protect the environment.*
Man muss *You must*		H: was helfen kann, die Natur zu erhalten. *which can help to preserve nature.*

Persönlich *Personally,*	benutze ich immer öffentliche Verkehrsmittel, *I always use public transport*	denn *because*	ich sorge mich um die Erde. *I worry about the Earth.*
Im Alltag *In my daily routine,*	sammle ich Müll von den Straßen, *I collect litter from the streets*		ich will umweltfreundlicher sein. *I want to be more environmentally friendly.*
	H: trenne ich den Müll, *I separate waste*		

Wenn wir *If we*	die Umwelt weiter verschmutzen, *pollute the environment further,*	werden die Temperaturen steigen. *temperatures will increase.*
Wenn die Leute *If people*	die Gefahren nicht verstehen, *don't understand the dangers,*	werden Tierarten verschwinden. *types of animals will disappear.*
H: Wenn Regierungen *If governments*	Higher: nicht für eine Lösung kämpfen, *don't fight for a solution,*	
	Higher: keine Verantwortung annehmen, *don't accept responsibility,*	

I'm trying to think of a joke about trees, but I'm stumped...

Think about your local area — what can people do to protect the environment there?

Nouns, Cases and Linking Words

Articles

der, die, das	*the (m, f, n — nom.)*
die	*the (plu. — nom.)*
ein, eine	*a / an (m/n, f — nom.)*
kein, keine	*no (m/n, f — nom.)*
keine	*no (plu. — nom.)*

Subject Pronouns

ich	*I*
du	*you (inf. sing.)*
er	*he, it (m)*
sie	*she, it (f)*
es	*it (n)*
man	*one, you, people in general*
wir	*we*
ihr	*you (inf. plu.)*
Sie	*you (frml. sing. & plu.)*
sie	*they*
selbst, selber	*self*

Direct Object Pronouns

mich	*me*
dich	*you (inf. sing.)*
ihn	*him, it (m)*
sie	*her, it (f)*
es	*it (n)*
Sie	*you (frml. sing.)*
einen	*one*

Higher

uns	*us*
euch	*you (inf. plu.)*
Sie	*you (frml. plu.)*
sie	*them*

Indirect Object Pronouns

mir	*me*
dir	*you (inf. sing.)*
ihm	*him, it (m)*
ihr	*her, it (f)*
ihm	*it (n)*
Ihnen	*you (frml. sing.)*
einem	*one*

Higher

uns	*us*
euch	*you (inf. plu.)*
Ihnen	*you (frml. plu.)*
ihnen	*them*

Indefinite Pronouns

jemand	*someone*
niemand	*no one*
etwas	*something, some*
alles	*everything, all*
nichts	*nothing*
alle (plu.)	*everyone, everybody*
andere	*other, different*
beide	*both, the two*
einer	*(some)one*

Higher

irgendein(e)	*some, any*
irgendetwas, irgendwas	*something, anything*
mehrere	*several, multiple, various*

Demonstrative Pronouns

solch	*such*
derselbe, dieselbe, dasselbe	*the same (one, ones)*

H

derjenige, diejenige, dasjenige	*the one (who, that)*

Relative and Interrogative Pronouns

der, die, das	*that, which, who (m, f, n)*
die	*that, which, who (plu.)*
wer?	*who? (nom.)*

H

was	*which, that*
wo	*where*

Accusative Reflexive Pronouns

mich	*myself*
dich	*yourself (inf. sing.)*
sich	*himself, herself, itself*
uns	*ourselves*
euch	*yourselves (inf. plu.)*
sich	*yourself (frml. sing.), yourselves (frml. plu.), themselves*

Dative Reflexive Pronouns

Higher

mir	*myself*
dir	*yourself (inf. sing.)*
sich	*himself, herself, itself*
uns	*ourselves*
euch	*yourselves (inf. plu.)*
sich	*yourself (frml. sing.), yourselves (frml. plu.), themselves*

Coordinating Conjunctions

und	*and*
oder	*or*
aber	*but, however*
denn	*because*

H

sondern	*(but) rather*

Subordinating Conjunctions

weil	*because*
wenn	*when, if, whenever*
als	*when, as*
obwohl	*although*
dass	*that*
nachdem	*after*
bevor	*before*
während	*while, whereas*
da	*as, because, since, given that*

Higher

ob	*whether, if*
damit	*so that*
indem	*while, by*
falls	*in case, if*
solange	*as long as*
sobald	*as soon as*
seitdem	*since*

Compound Conjunctions

entweder ... oder	*either ... or*
weder ... noch	*neither ... nor*
sowohl ... als auch	*both ... and*

Higher

Accusative Case Prepositions

durch	*through*
für	*for*
ohne	*without*
bis	*until, till, up to, by*
gegen	*against*
um	*at (o' clock), around*
pro	*per*

Dative Case Prepositions

mit	*with, by*
von	*from, of*
nach	*to, towards, after, according to*
zu	*to*
ab	*from, as of*
seit	*since, for*
außer	*except, apart from*
gegenüber	*opposite, across from*
aus	*out, out of, from*
bei	*at (the house of), with*
H laut	*according to*

Dual Case Prepositions

an	*on, at*
auf	*on, onto, at, to*
in	*in, into*
hinter	*behind*
neben	*next to, beside*
über	*about, above, over*
unter	*under, below, among*
zwischen	*between*
vor	*in front of, before, ago*
H entlang	*along*

Genitive Case Prepositions

Higher

trotz	*in spite of*
statt	*instead of*
währen	*during*
wegen	*because of*

Contracted Forms

am	*on the, at the (m/n — dat.)*
ans	*on(to) the, at the (n — acc.)*
im	*in the (m/n — dat.)*
ins	*into the (n — acc.)*
beim	*at the, with the (m/n)*
vom	*from the, of the (m/n)*
zur	*to the (f)*
zum	*to the (m/n)*

Prepositional Pronouns

darauf, drauf	*on it/them, to it/them*
damit	*with it/them*
dafür	*for it/that/them*
davon	*from it/them about it/them*

Higher

dadurch	*through it, as a result, as a consequence*
dahinter	*behind it*
daneben	*next to it, beside it*
daraus	*out of it, from it*
darin, drin, drinnen	*in it, in there, inside*
darüber, drüber	*above it, about it*
dazu	*to that, for that*
darunter	*under it, underneath*
dabei	*with it, there*
daran, dran	*on it, at it, in the process of it*
danach	*after it, afterwards*
dagegen	*against it, on the other hand*
darum	*around it, therefore*
davor	*before (it), in front of it*
dazwischen	*in between, between (them), among (them)*
daher	*from there, therefore*

Higher

worauf	*on what, to what*
womit	*with which*
wofür	*for what*
wovon	*from what, about what*
wodurch	*how, through which, as a result of which*
wohinter	*behind what*
woneben	*next to what, beside what*
woraus	*from what, from which*
worin	*in what, into what*
worüber	*what about*
wozu	*on what, onto what, at what, to what*
worunter	*under which, under what*
wobei	*in the process of which, with which, during which*
woran	*on what, at what*
wonach	*what … for, what … of*
wogegen	*against what, whereas*
worum	*about what*
wovor	*what … of, what … in front of*
wozwischen	*between what, between which*

Adjectives and Adverbs

Possessive Adjectives

mein	*my*
dein	*your (inf. sing.)*
sein	*his, its (m)*
ihr	*her, its (f)*
sein	*its (n)*
unser	*our*
euer	*your (inf. plu.)*
Ihr	*your (frml. sing. & plu.)*
ihr	*their*

Adverbs

schon	*already, yet*
gern, gerne	*gladly*
nicht	*not*
selbst	*even*
so	*so, in this way, thus, such*
sehr	*very, very much*
ganz	*quite*
etwas	*somewhat*
viel	*a lot*
meistens	*mostly*
mindestens	*at least, minimum*
wenigstens	*at least*
leider	*unfortunately, sadly*

Higher

vorher	*beforehand, earlier, previously*
bereits	*already*
nun	*now, well*
je	*ever, each*
vorbei	*past, over*
seitdem	*since then*
zunächst	*first, at first, to begin with, for now, for the time being*
eher	*earlier, sooner, rather*
erst	*first, only, not until*
bisher	*until now, up to now, yet, so far*
glücklicherweise	*fortunately, luckily*
stattdessen	*instead*
überhaupt	*at all, anyway*
unbedingt	*absolutely*
allerdings	*though, indeed, certainly*
ebenfalls	*likewise, also, as well, too*
jedenfalls	*in any case, at any rate, anyhow*
zumindest	*at least*
außerdem	*besides, in addition, furthermore*

dazu	*in addition, furthermore, besides*
zwar	*admittedly, to be precise, indeed*
etwa	*about, approximately*
eben	*just, now*
kaum	*hardly*
sowieso	*anyway*
teilweise	*partly, partially*
sogar	*even, in fact, actually*
doch	*however, but*
sonst	*otherwise, else*
übrigens	*by the way*
hin	*there*
her	*from something, ago*

Comparative Adjectives and Adverbs

als	*than*
so... wie	*as... as*
genauso... wie	*just as... as*
mehr	*more*
besser	*better*
höher	*higher, taller*
lieber	*more gladly, rather*

Superlative Adjectives

der beste	*the best*
der höchste	*the highest*
der meiste	*the most*
der nächste	*the next, nearest*

Superlative Adverbs

am besten	*(the) best*
am höchsten	*(the) highest*
am liebsten	*(the) most preferred, most preferably, rather*
am meisten	*(the) most*
am nächsten	*(the) next, nearest*

Notes

Notes

Notes

Progress Chart

Use this handy grid to track how you feel about each section.

Vocabulary Book Progress			
Section One — General Stuff			
Section Two — Identity & Relationships with Others			
Section Three — Healthy Living and Lifestyle			
Section Four — Education			
Section Five — Future Study and Work			
Section Six — Free-time Activities			
Section Seven — Customs, Festivals and Celebrations			
Section Eight — Celebrity Culture			
Section Nine — Travel and Tourism			
Section Ten — Media and Technology			
Section Eleven — Where People Live			
Section Twelve — Environmental and Social Issues			
Section Thirteen — Nouns, Cases and Linking Words			
Section Fourteen — Adjectives and Adverbs			

DAHV41